AF687857

From Distressed to Deluxe: Airbnb Property Flipping Strategies for Investors

"Breaking Into Short-Term Rental Investing"

Clyde N. Cook, III

© 2023 Clyde N. Cook, III All rights reserved. No part of this book may be reproduced or transmitted in any form or by any means, electronic or mechanical, including photocopying, recording, or by any information storage and retrieval system, without written permission from the author, except for the inclusion of brief quotations in a review. First Edition.

Table Of Contents

Chapter 1: Introduction to Airbnb Property Flipping

Understanding the Concept of Airbnb Property Flipping

In the world of real estate investment, there are numerous strategies that can yield lucrative returns. One such strategy that has gained significant traction in recent years is Airbnb property flipping. This subchapter aims to provide real estate investors with a comprehensive understanding of this concept, specifically focusing on purchasing distressed properties, renovating them, and then listing them on Airbnb for short-term rentals.

Airbnb property flipping involves identifying distressed properties that have the potential for transformation into desirable short-term rental accommodations. These distressed properties may be in need of repairs, have outdated designs, or be located in underdeveloped areas. The key to successful Airbnb property flipping lies in the ability to envision the property's potential and execute a renovation plan that will maximize its appeal to potential guests.

The first step in this process is identifying distressed properties with potential. Real estate investors must conduct thorough research and due diligence to find properties that are undervalued and have the potential for significant appreciation. This may involve networking with local real estate agents, attending foreclosure auctions, or leveraging online platforms that specialize in distressed property listings.

Once an ideal property has been identified, the next step is to plan and execute a renovation strategy that caters to the needs and preferences of Airbnb guests. This may include upgrading the property's amenities, improving its functionality, enhancing its aesthetics, or even expanding its capacity to accommodate more guests. The goal is to create a space that offers a unique and memorable experience for guests, ultimately leading to positive reviews and increased occupancy rates.

When it comes to listing the renovated property on Airbnb, real estate investors must employ effective marketing strategies to attract potential guests. This may involve professional photography, well-crafted property descriptions, competitive pricing, and strategic positioning within the Airbnb search algorithm. It is crucial to highlight the property's unique features, such as its location, amenities, or nearby attractions, to entice prospective guests to book their stay.

Airbnb property flipping can be a highly profitable investment strategy, especially for real estate investors who possess a keen eye for property potential and are willing to invest time and resources into the renovation process. By understanding the concept of Airbnb property flipping and implementing effective strategies, investors can transform distressed properties into deluxe accommodations that generate substantial returns through short-term rentals.

In conclusion, this subchapter has provided real estate investors with a comprehensive understanding of Airbnb property flipping. It has explored the process of purchasing distressed properties, renovating them, and listing them on Airbnb for short-term rentals. By leveraging this concept and implementing effective strategies, investors can tap into a lucrative market and achieve significant financial success through Airbnb property flipping.

Benefits and Challenges of Airbnb Property Flipping

In the ever-evolving world of real estate investment, Airbnb property flipping has emerged as a lucrative opportunity for savvy investors. This subchapter explores the benefits and challenges associated with this unique strategy, aimed specifically at real estate investors interested in purchasing distressed properties, renovating them, and then listing them on Airbnb for short-term rentals.

One of the most significant benefits of Airbnb property flipping is the potential for high returns on investment. By purchasing distressed properties at a lower price, investors have the opportunity to renovate and transform them into desirable short-term rentals, commanding premium rates. This strategy allows investors to capitalize on the rising popularity of Airbnb and tap into a growing market of travelers seeking unique and personalized accommodations.

Furthermore, Airbnb property flipping offers a flexible and dynamic investment approach. Unlike traditional long-term rentals, short-term rentals on Airbnb allow investors to adjust their pricing and availability based on market demand. This flexibility can lead to increased profitability as investors can take advantage of peak seasons and adjust rates accordingly.

Additionally, Airbnb property flipping presents an opportunity for investors to exercise their creativity and design skills. Renovating distressed properties to create stylish and inviting spaces can be a fulfilling and rewarding experience. The ability to infuse personal touches and unique design elements can attract discerning travelers and set properties apart from the competition.

However, along with the benefits come certain challenges that investors must be prepared to face. One of the main challenges is the increased competition in the Airbnb market. As the popularity of short-term rentals continues to grow, more investors are entering the market, making it crucial to differentiate properties and provide exceptional guest experiences to stay competitive.

Another challenge is the management of properties. Unlike traditional long-term rentals, short-term rentals require constant attention, including guest communication, cleaning, and maintenance. Investors must be prepared to either dedicate their time or hire a reliable property management service to handle these responsibilities effectively.

Lastly, regulatory compliance and legal considerations can pose challenges in some locations. It is essential for investors to thoroughly research and understand local regulations regarding short-term rentals to avoid legal issues and potential penalties.

In conclusion, Airbnb property flipping presents real estate investors with an exciting opportunity to capitalize on the rising popularity of short-term rentals. The benefits of high returns, flexibility, and creative freedom make this strategy appealing. However, investors must also be aware of the challenges of increased competition, property management, and regulatory compliance. By carefully navigating these challenges, investors can turn distressed properties into deluxe short-term rentals and achieve long-term success in this niche market.

Target Audience for this Book

The target audience for "From Distressed to Deluxe: Airbnb Property Flipping Strategies for Investors" is for real estate investors who are specifically interested in Airbnb property flipping. This book is tailored to those investors who are keen on purchasing distressed properties, renovating them, and then listing them on Airbnb for short-term rentals.

Real estate investors who are looking to tap into the lucrative market of Airbnb property flipping will find this book to be an invaluable resource. Whether you are a seasoned investor or just starting out in the real estate industry, this book will provide you with the essential strategies, tips, and techniques to successfully navigate the world of Airbnb property flipping.

This book is ideal for investors who are interested in the niche of Airbnb property flipping. It caters to those who understand the potential profitability of purchasing distressed properties at a lower cost, renovating them to a high standard, and then leveraging the power of Airbnb to generate substantial short-term rental income.

The target audience for this book is also comprised of individuals who are looking for alternative investment opportunities in the real estate market. Airbnb property flipping offers a unique avenue for investors to diversify their portfolio and capitalize on the growing demand for short-term rentals.

Additionally, this book is suitable for investors who are interested in both the financial and creative aspects of real estate. It provides insights into the financial calculations and considerations involved in identifying profitable properties, estimating renovation costs, and projecting rental income. Moreover, it explores the creative side of property flipping, such as design and staging tips to maximize the appeal of your Airbnb listings.

Ultimately, the target audience for "From Distressed to Deluxe: Airbnb Property Flipping Strategies for Investors" consists of real estate investors who are ready to take advantage of the booming short-term rental market through the purchase, renovation, and listing of distressed properties on Airbnb. This book will equip them with the knowledge, tools, and techniques needed to succeed in this niche and transform distressed properties into deluxe rentals.

Chapter 2: Getting Started with Airbnb Property Flipping

Researching the Real Estate Market

One of the key steps in successfully flipping distressed properties for Airbnb rentals is conducting thorough research on the real estate market. As a real estate investor in the niche of Airbnb property flipping, it is crucial to have a deep understanding of the market dynamics, trends, and opportunities to make informed decisions and maximize your profits.

To begin your research, it is essential to evaluate the demand for short-term rentals in your target location. Look for areas with a high influx of tourists, business travelers, or students, as these are potential sources of Airbnb bookings. Consider factors such as proximity to tourist attractions, universities, convention centers, or corporate headquarters, as these can significantly impact rental demand.

Next, analyze the competition in the area. Evaluate the existing Airbnb listings and identify gaps or opportunities that you can leverage. Look for unique selling points that can set your property apart from others, such as amenities, design, or location advantages. This research will help you determine the optimal pricing strategy and identify ways to attract potential guests.

Furthermore, researching the local regulations and zoning laws is essential. Some cities and neighborhoods have specific regulations governing short-term rentals, including licensing requirements, occupancy limits, or restrictions on certain types of properties. Ensure that you comply with all legal requirements to avoid any potential legal issues or fines.

Additionally, it is crucial to stay updated on the latest market trends and changes. Follow real estate news, attend industry conferences, and join online forums to connect with other real estate investors. This will provide you with valuable insights, tips, and strategies shared by experienced professionals in the field.

Lastly, consider partnering with local real estate agents who specialize in short-term rentals or Airbnb management companies. These professionals have extensive knowledge of the local market and can provide valuable advice on property selection, renovation ideas, and pricing strategies. Building a network of reliable partners will not only save you time and effort but also increase your chances of success in the competitive Airbnb property flipping market.

In conclusion, researching the real estate market is a crucial step for real estate investors specializing in Airbnb property flipping. By understanding the rental demand, competition, regulations, and market trends, you can make informed decisions and maximize your profits. Stay proactive, network with industry professionals, and keep up to date with market changes to stay ahead in this dynamic and lucrative niche.

Identifying Distressed Properties

In the world of real estate investing, finding the right properties is a crucial step towards building a successful portfolio. One strategy that has gained significant popularity among investors is Airbnb property flipping - the process of purchasing distressed properties, renovating them, and then listing them on Airbnb for short-term rentals. However, finding these distressed properties can be the key to unlocking incredible profit potential.

Identifying distressed properties requires a keen eye and an understanding of the market. These properties are often in poor condition, neglected, or facing financial distress. Real estate investors specializing in Airbnb property flipping can benefit greatly from targeting distressed properties, as they offer opportunities for significant value appreciation.

To begin your journey into identifying distressed properties, start by researching local market conditions. Look for areas that have a high demand for short-term rentals and a low supply of available properties. This will help you identify potential hotspots where distressed properties may exist.

Next, tap into your network of real estate professionals, including agents, brokers, and contractors. These individuals often have insider knowledge about distressed properties that are not yet listed on the market. By building relationships and networking within the industry, you can gain access to off-market distressed properties before they become widely available.

Additionally, keep a close eye on public foreclosure listings, auctions, and tax sales. These resources can provide valuable information about distressed properties that are in the process of being repossessed or sold due to financial difficulties. Attending these events or working with a knowledgeable agent can help you navigate the complex world of distressed property sales.

When evaluating distressed properties, it's important to conduct thorough due diligence. Assess the property's condition, potential renovation costs, and any legal or financial issues that may arise. This will help you accurately estimate the property's value and potential return on investment.

Remember, identifying distressed properties is just the first step in the Airbnb property flipping journey. Once you've acquired a distressed property, you'll need to develop a renovation strategy that will appeal to the short-term rental market. This may involve updating the property's amenities, improving its curb appeal, or enhancing its overall functionality.

In conclusion, identifying distressed properties is a crucial skill for real estate investors specializing in Airbnb property flipping. By researching market conditions, networking with professionals, and exploring foreclosure listings, you can uncover hidden gems with immense profit potential. Always conduct thorough due diligence and develop a renovation strategy that aligns with the demands of the short-term rental market. With the right approach, distressed properties can be transformed from dilapidated structures to deluxe Airbnb listings, generating substantial returns on your investment.

Evaluating Profit Potential

When it comes to Airbnb property flipping, evaluating profit potential is a crucial step that every real estate investor must master. The success of your venture relies heavily on your ability to determine whether a distressed property has the potential to be transformed into a deluxe space that will thrive in the Airbnb market. In this subchapter, we will explore the key factors to consider when evaluating profit potential in the realm of Airbnb property flipping.

Location is everything in real estate, and it holds true for Airbnb property flipping as well. A prime location can make all the difference between a property that attracts a steady stream of guests and one that remains vacant. Before making any purchase, thoroughly research the neighborhood, assessing its proximity to popular tourist attractions, transportation hubs, and local amenities. A property that is conveniently located will have a higher demand, leading to increased occupancy rates and, ultimately, greater profit potential.

Beyond location, it's crucial to evaluate the property's current condition and potential for renovation. Look for distressed properties that have strong bones and are in need of cosmetic improvements rather than extensive structural repairs. Conduct a thorough inspection to identify any underlying issues that could impact your renovation budget. Calculating an accurate estimate of renovation costs will help you determine if the property's profit potential aligns with your investment goals.

Furthermore, consider the local regulations and restrictions on short-term rentals in the area. Some cities have strict regulations that limit the number of days a property can be rented out on platforms like Airbnb. Familiarize yourself with these rules to ensure compliance and avoid any potential legal issues that could hamper your profitability.

An essential aspect of evaluating profit potential is conducting a market analysis. Research the current Airbnb market in the area, analyzing occupancy rates, average daily rates, and competition. Understanding the local demand and supply dynamics will provide valuable insights into the potential profitability of your Airbnb property flipping venture.

Lastly, consider the scalability of your business. Evaluate whether you have the resources and bandwidth to manage multiple properties simultaneously. Scaling your Airbnb property flipping business can significantly increase your profit potential, as it allows you to leverage economies of scale and diversify your income streams.

In conclusion, evaluating profit potential is a critical skill for real estate investors specializing in Airbnb property flipping. By carefully assessing location, property condition, renovation costs, local regulations, market dynamics, and scalability, you can make informed decisions that maximize your chances of success in this niche market. Remember, thorough evaluation is the key to transforming distressed properties into deluxe Airbnb spaces that generate substantial returns on your investment.

Creating a Budget and Financial Plan

When it comes to successfully flipping distressed properties for Airbnb rentals, it is crucial for real estate investors to have a well-thought-out budget and financial plan in place. This subchapter will guide you through the process of creating a comprehensive budget that includes all the necessary expenses and helps you maximize your return on investment.

First and foremost, it is important to assess the total cost of purchasing a distressed property and renovating it to meet the standards of an Airbnb rental. This includes the purchase price, closing costs, any necessary repairs or renovations, as well as staging and furnishing costs. By accurately estimating these expenses, you can determine the initial investment required and set a realistic budget.

Next, consider the ongoing expenses that will be incurred once the property is listed on Airbnb. These may include mortgage payments, property taxes, insurance, utilities, cleaning and maintenance costs, as well as marketing and management fees if you choose to outsource these tasks. By accounting for these expenses, you can establish a monthly budget and assess the profitability of your Airbnb rental.

In addition to expenses, it is essential to project the potential revenue generated from your Airbnb property. Conduct market research to determine the average rental rates in your area and evaluate the occupancy rate of similar properties. This will help you estimate the potential income your property can generate and make informed decisions about pricing and rental strategies.

A financial plan should also include contingency funds for unexpected expenses or vacancies. It is wise to set aside a portion of your budget for emergencies or any unforeseen circumstances that may arise during the flipping or rental process.

Regularly reviewing and adjusting your budget and financial plan is crucial to ensure the long-term success of your Airbnb property flipping venture. Keep track of your actual expenses and revenues, and compare them to your projected figures. This will allow you to identify any areas where you may need to make adjustments and optimize your financial performance.

Remember, creating a budget and financial plan is not a one-time task but an ongoing process. By staying organized and informed, you can make sound financial decisions and maximize your profitability in the competitive world of Airbnb property flipping.

Chapter 3: Purchasing Distressed Properties

Locating Distressed Properties

Finding distressed properties is the first crucial step in the process of Airbnb property flipping. These properties, often in poor condition or facing financial difficulties, present a unique opportunity for real estate investors to turn them into profitable short-term rentals. In this subchapter, we will explore various strategies and techniques to help you locate these hidden gems and capitalize on their potential.

One effective method for finding distressed properties is through networking within the real estate community. Attending local real estate investment meetups, joining online forums, and connecting with other investors can provide valuable insights and leads. Experienced investors often have access to off-market distressed properties or can refer you to reliable sources.

Another approach is to establish relationships with real estate agents specializing in distressed properties. These professionals have access to exclusive listings and can notify you when potential deals arise. By clearly communicating your investment goals and criteria, agents can help narrow down the search and save you time.

Utilizing online platforms and technology can also enhance your search for distressed properties. Websites such as foreclosure.com, Auction.com, and RealtyTrac provide extensive databases of distressed properties across the country. These platforms allow you to filter properties based on location, price range, and specific distress factors, providing a convenient way to identify potential investments.

Driving through neighborhoods and looking for physical signs of distress, such as overgrown lawns, boarded-up windows, or "For Sale" signs, can also lead to promising opportunities. Additionally, reaching out to local property owners directly or sending out targeted mailers can yield favorable results. It is important to approach owners with empathy and understanding, as they may be experiencing challenging circumstances.

Furthermore, partnering with professionals in related fields, such as contractors, property managers, or wholesalers, can provide valuable leads on distressed properties. These individuals often have insider knowledge of properties in need of repair or financial assistance and can offer valuable insights into potential investment opportunities.

In conclusion, locating distressed properties is a crucial aspect of Airbnb property flipping. By leveraging networking, real estate agents, online platforms, physical observation, direct outreach, and partnerships, real estate investors can uncover hidden opportunities and capitalize on their potential for profitable short-term rentals. Remember to conduct thorough due diligence and carefully evaluate each property before making any investment decisions.

Negotiating the Purchase Price

In the competitive world of real estate investing, negotiating the purchase price of a distressed property is a crucial skill that can make or break your Airbnb property flipping business. As a real estate investor specializing in purchasing distressed properties, renovating them, and then listing them on Airbnb for short-term rentals, understanding the art of negotiation is essential to ensure profitability and success.

When it comes to negotiating the purchase price, it's important to remember that knowledge is power. Before entering into any negotiations, conduct thorough research on the property, its market value, and comparable sales in the area. This will provide you with a solid foundation of information that you can leverage during the negotiation process.

One effective strategy is to approach negotiations with a win-win mindset. While you aim to secure the property at the lowest possible price, it's also important to consider the seller's perspective and find mutually beneficial solutions. Building rapport and establishing a positive relationship with the seller can increase your chances of reaching a favorable agreement.

Another key aspect of negotiating the purchase price is understanding the seller's motivation. Distressed properties often come with their own set of challenges, ranging from financial difficulties to time constraints. By empathizing with the seller's situation and identifying their motivations, you can tailor your negotiation strategy accordingly. For example, if the seller is in urgent need of cash, you may have a stronger position to negotiate a lower purchase price.

Additionally, be prepared to showcase your expertise and highlight the value you can bring to the property. As an experienced Airbnb property flipper, emphasize your track record of successfully renovating and maximizing the rental potential of distressed properties. This can instill confidence in the seller and potentially lead to more flexible negotiations.

Lastly, don't be afraid to walk away if the negotiation doesn't align with your goals. It's important to have a clear understanding of your investment criteria and stick to it. Sometimes, walking away from a deal that doesn't meet your requirements can open doors to even better opportunities in the future.

Negotiating the purchase price of distressed properties for your Airbnb property flipping business requires a combination of knowledge, strategy, and effective communication skills. By approaching negotiations with a win-win mindset, understanding the seller's motivations, and showcasing your expertise, you can increase your chances of securing favorable deals and achieving long-term success in the competitive real estate market.

Conducting Due Diligence

Before embarking on any investment journey, it is crucial for real estate investors, particularly those interested in Airbnb property flipping, to conduct thorough due diligence. This process involves evaluating and analyzing potential distressed properties to ensure they align with your investment goals and yield maximum returns. By dedicating time and effort to this crucial step, investors can minimize risks and make informed decisions. In this subchapter, we will explore the essential aspects of conducting due diligence for Airbnb property flipping.

Firstly, it is important to identify your investment criteria and objectives. Are you looking for distressed properties in a specific location? What is your budget for renovation and acquisition costs? Defining your investment criteria will help streamline your search and narrow down potential properties that align with your goals.

Next, research the local real estate market and Airbnb regulations in your target area. Understanding the demand for short-term rentals, occupancy rates, and any legal restrictions will provide valuable insights for your investment strategy. Additionally, consider economic factors, such as job growth, tourism, and infrastructure development, as they can impact the profitability of your investment.

When evaluating distressed properties, thoroughly examine their physical condition. Engage professionals, such as inspectors and contractors, to assess the property's structural integrity, electrical systems, plumbing, and overall renovation requirements. This will enable you to estimate the costs involved accurately and avoid any surprises during the flipping process.

Furthermore, review the property's financials, including its current and potential rental income, operating expenses, and any outstanding liens or debts. This information will help you determine the property's profitability and ensure you make a sound investment decision.

Additionally, consider the potential risks associated with Airbnb property flipping. Analyze factors such as seasonality, competition, and potential changes in local regulations that could impact short-term rental operations. By understanding and mitigating these risks, you can proactively protect your investment and maximize returns.

Finally, consult with experienced professionals, such as real estate agents, attorneys, and accountants, who can provide valuable guidance throughout the due diligence process. Their expertise can help you navigate legal complexities, negotiate favorable terms, and ensure compliance with local regulations.

In conclusion, conducting thorough due diligence is a crucial step for real estate investors interested in Airbnb property flipping. By carefully evaluating potential distressed properties, considering market conditions, assessing financials, and mitigating risks, investors can make informed decisions and maximize their returns. Remember, a well-executed due diligence process sets the foundation for successful Airbnb property flipping ventures.

Financing Options for Distressed Property Purchases

When it comes to Airbnb property flipping, one of the crucial steps is finding the right financing options for purchasing distressed properties. These properties, often in need of renovation or repair, can present excellent investment opportunities for real estate investors. However, securing financing for such purchases requires careful consideration and knowledge of the available options. In this subchapter, we will explore various financing avenues tailored specifically for the niche of Airbnb property flipping.

1. Traditional Bank Loans: Real estate investors can approach traditional banks for loans to finance their distressed property purchases. However, it's important to note that banks typically have strict lending criteria, making it challenging to secure loans for distressed properties. Investors must have a strong credit score, a substantial down payment, and a solid business plan to increase their chances of approval.

2. Hard Money Loans: Hard money loans are often a popular choice for investors in the Airbnb property flipping niche. These loans are provided by private lenders or companies that specialize in financing real estate investments. Hard money loans usually have higher interest rates and shorter terms, but they offer flexibility and a faster approval process compared to traditional banks.

3. Private Investors: Real estate investors can seek funding from private investors who are interested in diversifying their investment portfolios. Private investors may be willing to provide the necessary funds for purchasing distressed properties in exchange for a share of the profits or a fixed interest rate. Building relationships with potential private investors through networking events or real estate investment clubs can lead to fruitful financing opportunities.

4. Crowdfunding: With the rise of real estate crowdfunding platforms, investors now have access to a pool of potential lenders interested in funding property purchases. These platforms allow multiple investors to contribute smaller amounts, collectively financing the property purchase. Crowdfunding can be an effective way to secure financing for distressed property purchases, especially for investors who may not qualify for traditional bank loans.

5. Seller Financing: In some cases, distressed property owners may be open to providing financing options themselves. This arrangement, known as seller financing or owner financing, allows investors to make a down payment and then pay the remaining balance directly to the property owner over an agreed-upon period. This option can be beneficial for investors who are unable to secure traditional financing or who prefer to bypass the lengthy loan approval process.

Before diving into distressed property purchases, real estate investors in the Airbnb property flipping niche must thoroughly research and understand the financing options available to them. Each option has its own advantages and disadvantages, and investors should carefully evaluate their financial circumstances and investment goals to determine the most suitable financing option for their needs. By choosing the right financing strategy, investors can confidently embark on their journey from distressed to deluxe, maximizing their Airbnb property flipping profits.

Chapter 4: Renovating and Rehabilitating the Property

Developing a Renovation Plan

In the world of real estate investment, one of the most lucrative niches is Airbnb property flipping. This strategy involves purchasing distressed properties, renovating them, and then listing them on Airbnb for short-term rentals. However, the success of this venture heavily relies on having a well-thought-out renovation plan. In this subchapter, we will delve into the crucial steps involved in developing a renovation plan that will transform distressed properties into deluxe accommodations.

The first step in developing a renovation plan is conducting a thorough property analysis. This entails assessing the current condition of the property, identifying any structural or cosmetic issues, and determining the areas that require the most attention. By taking a comprehensive approach, real estate investors can develop a renovation plan that not only addresses the property's shortcomings but also enhances its appeal to potential guests.

Once the property analysis is complete, the next step is to set a realistic budget and timeline. This involves determining the scope of the renovation, estimating the costs of materials and labor, and establishing a timeline for completing the project. It is crucial to strike a balance between the desired level of renovation and the available budget to ensure a profitable outcome.

With the budget and timeline in place, the next step is to prioritize renovations based on their impact on guest experience and return on investment. For Airbnb properties, it is essential to create spaces that are not only aesthetically pleasing but also functional and comfortable. This may involve updating the kitchen and bathrooms, improving the overall layout, and creating inviting outdoor spaces.

Furthermore, real estate investors should consider incorporating smart home technology into their renovation plan. This can include features such as keyless entry systems, automated thermostats, and voice-activated assistants, which enhance the guest experience and attract tech-savvy travelers.

Lastly, it is crucial to work with reliable contractors and suppliers who can execute the renovation plan efficiently and within the allocated budget. Building a strong network of professionals in the industry will ensure that the renovation process runs smoothly and minimizes any potential setbacks.

In conclusion, developing a renovation plan is a critical step in the Airbnb property flipping strategy. By conducting a thorough property analysis, setting a realistic budget and timeline, prioritizing renovations, incorporating smart home technology, and working with reliable professionals, real estate investors can successfully transform distressed properties into deluxe accommodations. This subchapter has provided an overview of the key considerations for developing a renovation plan, setting the foundation for a profitable Airbnb property flipping venture.

Hiring Contractors and Managing Construction

One of the most critical aspects of the Airbnb property flipping process is the selection and management of contractors for the renovation and construction work. As real estate investors engaged in the niche of Airbnb property flipping – which involves purchasing distressed properties, renovating them, and then listing them on Airbnb for short-term rentals – finding reliable contractors is crucial to the success of your venture.

When it comes to hiring contractors, it is essential to conduct thorough research and due diligence. Seek recommendations from other investors in the real estate industry or local Airbnb hosts who have successfully completed similar projects. Look for contractors who have experience in remodeling distressed properties and are familiar with the specific needs and requirements of short-term rentals.

Before finalizing any contractor, be sure to interview multiple candidates and request estimates for the project. This will allow you to compare their pricing, quality of work, and estimated timelines. It is also vital to check their licensing, insurance, and past client references. By doing so, you can ensure that you are hiring a reputable contractor who is capable of completing the project to your satisfaction.

Once you have selected a contractor, communication and project management become crucial. Clearly communicate your expectations, budget constraints, and project deadlines. Regularly check in with the contractor to monitor progress and address any concerns or issues that may arise. Maintaining an open line of communication ensures that the project stays on track and any potential problems are addressed promptly.

Managing the construction process involves overseeing the quality of work, adherence to timelines, and budget control. Regular site visits will enable you to assess the progress, address any design changes or modifications, and ensure that the renovation aligns with your vision for the property. Monitoring the budget closely will help you avoid any cost overruns and ensure that the project remains financially viable.

In conclusion, hiring contractors and effectively managing construction is a crucial aspect of the Airbnb property flipping process. By conducting thorough research, interviewing multiple candidates, and maintaining open communication, you can ensure that your renovation project stays on track and yields the desired results. Remember, finding reliable contractors is key to transforming distressed properties into deluxe Airbnb rentals and maximizing your return on investment.

Selecting Materials and Finishes

When it comes to Airbnb property flipping, one of the key factors that can make or break your success is the selection of materials and finishes for your renovations. Choosing the right materials and finishes can not only enhance the overall appeal of your property but also ensure durability and ease of maintenance. In this subchapter, we will explore the essential considerations for selecting materials and finishes that will transform distressed properties into luxurious havens for Airbnb guests.

First and foremost, it is crucial to understand your target audience and the specific requirements of the short-term rental market. Real estate investors in the Airbnb property flipping niche should aim to create spaces that are not only aesthetically pleasing but also functional and durable. Opt for materials that are both visually appealing and able to withstand the wear and tear of frequent occupancy.

When selecting materials, focus on creating a cohesive design theme that reflects the desired ambiance of your property. Whether you aim for a modern, rustic, or eclectic style, consistency throughout the space is key. This includes choosing materials and finishes that complement each other, such as coordinating flooring, wall colors, and fixtures.

Consider using durable and low-maintenance materials that will save you time and money in the long run. For example, opt for hardwood or laminate flooring, which is not only visually appealing but also easy to clean and resistant to stains. In the kitchen and bathrooms, choose materials that are resistant to moisture and can withstand daily use, such as quartz or granite countertops and porcelain or ceramic tiles.

In addition to durability, it is essential to consider the environmental impact of the materials you choose. Many guests nowadays prioritize eco-friendly accommodations. Consider using sustainable materials, such as bamboo flooring or reclaimed wood, and low VOC (volatile organic compounds) paints and finishes, to appeal to this growing market segment.

Lastly, keep in mind the budget constraints of your Airbnb property flipping project. While it may be tempting to splurge on high-end materials and finishes, it is crucial to strike a balance between quality and cost. Look for cost-effective alternatives that offer a similar aesthetic appeal, such as vinyl plank flooring that mimics the look of hardwood.

In conclusion, selecting the right materials and finishes is a critical aspect of Airbnb property flipping. By considering the target audience, cohesive design, durability, sustainability, and budget, real estate investors can elevate distressed properties into luxurious havens that will attract Airbnb guests and maximize returns on investment.

Overcoming Common Renovation Challenges

Renovating distressed properties for Airbnb rentals can be a lucrative investment strategy for real estate investors. However, it is not without its challenges. In this subchapter, we will explore some common renovation challenges and provide valuable insights on how to overcome them.

One of the major challenges in property flipping for Airbnb rentals is the tight budget. Often, distressed properties require extensive renovations, and sticking to a limited budget can be tough. To overcome this challenge, it is crucial to carefully plan and prioritize the renovation tasks. Assess the property thoroughly and identify areas that require immediate attention. Focus on essential repairs and improvements that have a significant impact on the property's rental potential. By prioritizing wisely, you can ensure that your budget is allocated efficiently and effectively.

Another common challenge faced by real estate investors during the renovation process is finding reliable contractors and tradespeople. Working with inexperienced or unprofessional contractors can lead to delays, cost overruns, and subpar workmanship. To overcome this challenge, invest time in researching and vetting potential contractors. Seek recommendations from other investors or industry professionals. Conduct interviews, check references, and review their previous work. By partnering with trustworthy contractors, you can ensure that your renovation project progresses smoothly and meets your desired standards.

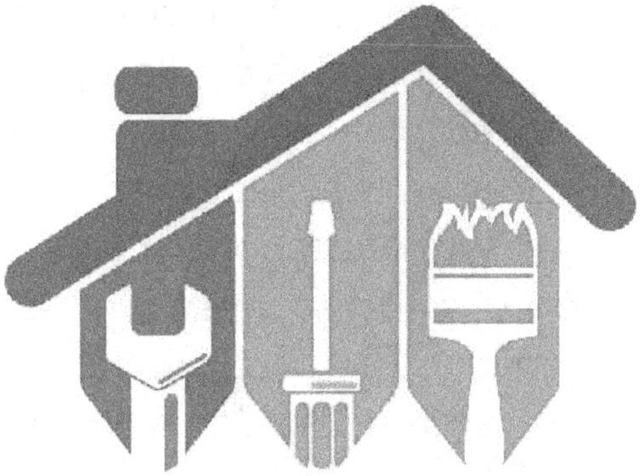

Additionally, navigating through local regulations and permits can be a daunting task for real estate investors. Each city or municipality may have specific requirements and guidelines for short-term rentals. It is essential to familiarize yourself with the local laws and regulations to avoid potential legal issues. Engage with local authorities or seek advice from experienced property flippers in the area to gain insights into the specific regulations that pertain to Airbnb rentals. By proactively addressing these regulatory challenges, you can ensure a seamless Airbnb property flipping process.

Lastly, managing project timelines and deadlines can be a significant challenge during property renovations. Delays can lead to increased carrying costs and lost rental income. To overcome this challenge, establish a detailed project plan with specific timelines for each renovation task. Regularly communicate with your contractors to monitor progress and address any potential delays proactively. Effective project management and timely decision-making are crucial for meeting deadlines and ensuring a successful Airbnb property flipping venture.

By understanding and proactively addressing these common renovation challenges, real estate investors can maximize their returns and successfully transform distressed properties into deluxe Airbnb rentals. With careful planning, diligent research, and strategic execution, you can unlock the full potential of your investment and thrive in the niche of Airbnb property flipping.

First and foremost, it is essential to comprehend the unique dynamics of the Airbnb market. Unlike traditional long-term rentals or hotels, Airbnb offers travelers a more personalized and authentic experience. The demand for unique and stylish accommodations has skyrocketed, presenting a golden opportunity for savvy real estate investors. By catering to this growing consumer trend, investors can tap into a lucrative market and generate substantial returns on their investment.

One of the crucial aspects of understanding the Airbnb market is identifying profitable locations and property types. Conducting thorough market research is essential to identify areas with high demand and limited supply, driving up rental rates and occupancy rates. Additionally, understanding the preferences of Airbnb travelers, such as proximity to tourist attractions, public transportation, and popular neighborhoods, will help investors target the right properties and optimize their rental income potential.

Chapter 5: Designing for Airbnb Rentals

Understanding the Airbnb Market

The Airbnb phenomenon has taken the real estate market by storm, revolutionizing the way people travel and experience new destinations. For real estate investors looking to capitalize on this booming market, understanding the intricacies of the Airbnb market is crucial. In this subchapter, we will delve into the key factors that define the Airbnb market and provide valuable insights for those interested in Airbnb property flipping: purchasing distressed properties, renovating them, and then listing them on Airbnb for short-term rentals.

Furthermore, renovating distressed properties is a fundamental step in the Airbnb property flipping strategy. Investing in quality renovations that enhance the property's aesthetics and functionality will attract more guests and command higher rental rates. Understanding the design trends and amenities that appeal to Airbnb travelers, such as modern kitchens, comfortable furnishings, and unique features, will give investors a competitive edge in the market.

To successfully navigate the Airbnb market, real estate investors must also consider the legal and regulatory aspects associated with short-term rentals. Familiarizing oneself with local laws, zoning restrictions, and permit requirements is crucial to avoid potential legal issues and ensure compliance. Engaging with local real estate agents, property managers, and legal professionals with expertise in the Airbnb market can provide valuable guidance and mitigate risks.

In conclusion, understanding the dynamics of the Airbnb market is paramount for real estate investors interested in Airbnb property flipping. By comprehending the unique demands and preferences of Airbnb travelers, identifying profitable locations, conducting quality renovations, and staying up-to-date with local regulations, investors can maximize their returns and build a successful Airbnb property flipping business. Stay tuned for the following chapters, where we will delve deeper into each aspect of this exciting investment strategy.

Creating a Unique and Attractive Rental Space

When it comes to Airbnb property flipping, one of the key factors that can make or break your success is creating a unique and attractive rental space. In the competitive world of short-term rentals, it is crucial to stand out from the crowd and offer something truly special to your guests. In this subchapter, we will explore some strategies and tips to help you transform distressed properties into deluxe Airbnb rentals that will wow your guests and maximize your profits.

First and foremost, it is essential to understand your target audience and the specific niche you are catering to. Are you targeting budget travelers, luxury seekers, or a specific theme such as eco-friendly or pet-friendly rentals? Knowing your audience will allow you to tailor your property renovations and amenities accordingly, ensuring that you provide a unique experience that meets their needs and desires.

To create an attractive rental space, pay close attention to the interior design and decor. Choose a cohesive theme or style that reflects the ambiance you want to create. Whether it's modern and minimalist, cozy and rustic, or vibrant and eclectic, consistency in design will leave a lasting impression on your guests. Consider hiring a professional interior designer or utilizing online resources to help you achieve the desired look.

Investing in high-quality furnishings and amenities is another essential aspect of creating a unique rental space. Comfortable beds, luxurious linens, and stylish furniture will make your guests feel pampered and enhance their overall experience. Additionally, consider adding special touches such as welcome baskets, personalized guest guides, or unique artwork to add a sense of charm and individuality to your property.

Beyond the interior, don't overlook the exterior of your rental space. Curb appeal plays a significant role in attracting guests. Enhance the landscaping, update the facade, and create inviting outdoor spaces such as patios or balconies where guests can relax and enjoy the surroundings. Attention to detail in every aspect of your property will make it stand out from the competition and generate positive reviews and repeat bookings.

Lastly, leverage technology to enhance the guest experience. Install smart home devices, such as keyless entry systems or voice-controlled assistants, to provide convenience and security. Invest in high-speed internet and entertainment options like streaming services or gaming consoles to keep your guests entertained during their stay.

By focusing on creating a unique and attractive rental space, you will position yourself as a top choice in the Airbnb market. Your attention to detail, stylish design, and thoughtful amenities will not only attract guests but also enable you to command higher rental rates. Remember, the key to success in Airbnb property flipping is to create properties that not only meet but exceed the expectations of your target audience.

Furnishing and Decorating for Maximum Appeal

When it comes to flipping properties for Airbnb rentals, one crucial aspect that can make or break your success is how you furnish and decorate the space. Creating an appealing and inviting atmosphere is key to attracting guests and generating positive reviews. In this subchapter, we will explore some strategies and tips to help you furnish and decorate your Airbnb property for maximum appeal.

First and foremost, it is important to understand your target audience. As real estate investors in the niche of Airbnb property flipping, your goal is to create a space that will appeal to short-term renters. Take some time to research the local market and understand the preferences and expectations of your potential guests. Are they primarily business travelers, vacationing families, or couples looking for a romantic getaway? Understanding your target market will help you make informed decisions when it comes to furnishing and decorating your property.

When selecting furniture, opt for pieces that are both stylish and functional. Consider investing in comfortable beds, quality linens, and ample storage options. Space-saving furniture, such as foldable tables and sleeper sofas, can be a great addition to maximize the use of smaller areas. Remember to choose durable materials that can withstand the wear and tear of frequent usage.

When it comes to decorating, aim for a cohesive and aesthetically pleasing look. Neutral color palettes are generally safe choices as they appeal to a wide range of tastes. However, don't be afraid to add pops of color or unique accents to create a memorable and Instagram-worthy space. Artwork, decorative pillows, and rugs can all add character and warmth to your property.

Additionally, pay attention to lighting in your Airbnb property. Natural light is highly valued by guests, so ensure that your space has ample windows or skylights. Supplement this with well-placed artificial lighting, including task lighting for work areas and soft ambient lighting for relaxation.

Lastly, don't forget about the finishing touches. Pay attention to details like fresh flowers, scented candles, and quality amenities. These small gestures can make a significant impact on guests, leaving a lasting impression and encouraging positive reviews.

In conclusion, furnishing and decorating your Airbnb property is not just about making it look pretty. It is about creating an inviting and comfortable space that will attract guests and generate positive reviews. By understanding your target audience, selecting functional furniture, creating a cohesive aesthetic, and paying attention to the finishing touches, you can ensure your Airbnb property stands out from the competition and maximizes its appeal to potential renters.

Incorporating Smart Home Technology

In today's digital age, smart home technology has become an essential aspect of modern living. Real estate investors who specialize in Airbnb property flipping can significantly enhance the value and appeal of their properties by incorporating smart home technology. This subchapter will explore the various ways in which investors can leverage smart home technology to attract more guests, increase rental rates, and ultimately maximize their return on investment.

One of the primary advantages of incorporating smart home technology into Airbnb properties is the convenience it offers to guests. By integrating devices such as smart thermostats, automated lighting systems, and voice-controlled assistants like Amazon Echo or Google Home, investors can provide guests with a seamless and intuitive experience. For instance, guests can easily adjust the temperature, control the lighting, and even play music or access local information using voice commands. These features not only enhance comfort but also create a modern and luxurious ambiance that appeals to discerning travelers.

Furthermore, smart home technology can greatly enhance the safety and security of Airbnb properties. Investing in smart locks allows guests to access the property using personalized codes or smartphone apps, eliminating the need for physical keys. This improves security by minimizing the risk of unauthorized access. Additionally, investors can install smart security cameras and smoke detectors, which can be monitored remotely to ensure the safety of guests and the property.

Another aspect to consider when incorporating smart home technology is energy efficiency. Smart thermostats and lighting systems can be programmed to optimize energy consumption, reducing utility costs and minimizing the property's carbon footprint. This eco-friendly approach not only appeals to environmentally conscious travelers but also helps investors save on operational expenses in the long run.

Lastly, real estate investors should consider the potential for automation and remote management that smart home technology offers. From remotely controlling access and monitoring security cameras to managing bookings and guest communication, investors can streamline operations and minimize the need for physical presence on-site. This scalability and flexibility are particularly beneficial for investors who manage multiple Airbnb properties, allowing them to efficiently oversee their portfolio from anywhere in the world.

Incorporating smart home technology into Airbnb property flipping strategies is a game-changer for real estate investors. By offering convenience, safety, energy efficiency, and automation, investors can differentiate their properties from the competition and attract a wider range of guests. As technology continues to evolve, embracing and leveraging smart home technology will be crucial for investors looking to stay ahead in the Airbnb market.

Chapter 6: Listing and Marketing on Airbnb

Optimizing your Airbnb Listing

When it comes to Airbnb property flipping, purchasing distressed properties, renovating them, and then listing them on Airbnb for short-term rentals can yield significant profits. However, in order to maximize your returns and attract more guests, it is crucial to optimize your Airbnb listing. In this subchapter, we will explore effective strategies to make your listing stand out and increase your chances of success in the competitive world of short-term rentals.

1. Captivating Title and Descriptive Introduction:
Craft a captivating title that accurately reflects the unique features of your property. Additionally, ensure your descriptive introduction highlights the key selling points, such as location, amenities, and any special features that make your property exceptional. Use engaging language and be specific to entice potential guests.

2. High-Quality Photos:
Invest in professional photography to showcase your property in the best light. Include a variety of high-quality photos that capture the different areas of your property. Pay attention to lighting, angles, and staging to create an inviting atmosphere that entices guests to book.

3. Highlight Unique Features:
Identify and emphasize the unique features of your property that set it apart from competitors. It could be a stunning view, a cozy fireplace, an outdoor entertainment area, or a luxurious spa. Make sure to mention these features in your description and showcase them in your photos.

Photo Courtesy of Endless Pool & Spas

4. Accurate and Detailed Amenities List:
Provide an accurate and comprehensive list of amenities available to guests, such as Wi-Fi, parking, kitchen appliances, and entertainment options. Be transparent about what guests can expect during their stay to avoid any misunderstandings or negative reviews.

5. Positive Guest Reviews:
Encourage guests to leave positive reviews by providing exceptional service, prompt communication, and a comfortable and clean space. Respond to reviews promptly and address any concerns or issues raised by guests. Positive reviews build trust and credibility, attracting more guests to your listing.

6. Competitive Pricing:
Research similar listings in your area to determine competitive pricing. Set your rates strategically, taking into consideration factors like location, seasonality, and local events. Offering competitive prices can attract more guests and increase your occupancy rate.

7. Constantly Update and Improve:
Regularly assess your listing to identify areas for improvement. Stay updated with the latest trends and guest preferences to make necessary adjustments. Continuously upgrade your property and amenities to provide an unforgettable experience for your guests.

By following these optimization strategies, you can enhance the appeal of your Airbnb listing and increase your chances of success in the Airbnb property flipping niche. Remember, attention to detail, exceptional service, and continuous improvement are key to attracting more guests and maximizing your profits.

Setting the Right Rental Rates

One of the key factors in successfully flipping distressed properties and listing them on Airbnb for short-term rentals is setting the right rental rates. Determining the ideal price for your property is crucial to attract guests while maximizing your profits as a real estate investor. In this subchapter, we will explore the strategies and considerations involved in setting rental rates that not only meet the market demand but also ensure a healthy return on investment.

To begin with, it is essential to research the local market and analyze the competition in your area. Understanding the going rates for similar properties listed on Airbnb will provide you with valuable insights into pricing trends and demand. Take note of factors such as location, amenities, and property size that influence rental rates. By evaluating these aspects, you can position your property competitively and adjust your rates accordingly.

Additionally, consider the seasonality of your location. Many Airbnb markets experience fluctuations in demand throughout the year, and adjusting your rates accordingly can maximize your occupancy rates. Analyzing historical booking data and local events can help you identify peak and off-peak seasons, allowing you to set higher rates during periods of high demand and lower rates during slower periods to attract more guests.

Another important consideration is the cost of managing your property. Calculate your expenses, including mortgage payments, property taxes, utilities, insurance, and any other maintenance or management fees. These costs should be factored into your rental rates to ensure you cover your expenses and generate a healthy profit.

Furthermore, keep in mind the value you offer to potential guests. Highlight unique features, amenities, and improvements you have made to your property that differentiate it from others in the market. Emphasizing these selling points can justify higher rental rates and attract guests who are willing to pay a premium for an exceptional experience.

Lastly, don't forget to regularly review and adjust your rental rates based on market dynamics, guest feedback, and seasonality. Continuously monitoring the market and staying updated on industry trends will allow you to optimize your pricing strategy and stay ahead of the competition.

In conclusion, setting the right rental rates is a critical aspect of successful Airbnb property flipping. By conducting thorough market research, considering seasonality, factoring in expenses, showcasing unique value propositions, and staying adaptable, real estate investors can maximize their profits while ensuring a steady stream of guests for their short-term rental properties.

Attracting Positive Reviews and Building a Strong Reputation

In the world of Airbnb property flipping, success is not solely dependent on acquiring distressed properties and renovating them to perfection. In fact, one of the most crucial aspects of this business model lies in attracting positive reviews and building a strong reputation. As real estate investors in the niche of Airbnb property flipping, it is essential to understand the power of positive reviews and their impact on your success.

Positive reviews are the lifeblood of your business. They not only encourage potential guests to choose your property over others but also help establish trust and credibility in the market. A strong reputation is built upon a foundation of excellent guest experiences, and this chapter will guide you on how to achieve just that.

Firstly, it is crucial to ensure that your property meets the highest standards of cleanliness, comfort, and functionality. Investing in quality furnishings, amenities, and thoughtful touches will go a long way in impressing your guests. Remember, the goal is to provide an experience that exceeds their expectations.

Secondly, effective communication plays a vital role in garnering positive reviews. Respond promptly to inquiries, be transparent about any potential issues or limitations of your property, and provide detailed instructions for check-in and check-out. By being attentive and responsive, you demonstrate your commitment to providing exceptional customer service.

Lastly, don't underestimate the power of social proof. Actively encourage satisfied guests to leave reviews and testimonials on your Airbnb listing. Consider offering incentives such as discounts or future booking credits to motivate guests to share their positive experiences. Positive reviews act as endorsements that can significantly impact potential guests' decision-making process.

Furthermore, consider going the extra mile to surprise and delight your guests. Small gestures like leaving a personalized welcome note, offering a local guidebook, or providing complimentary refreshments can leave a lasting impression. These thoughtful touches not only make the guest feel valued but also increase the chances of receiving a glowing review.

Equally important is managing any negative feedback you may receive. Addressing guest concerns promptly and professionally is vital to maintaining a strong reputation. Take the time to understand the issue, offer a solution, and follow up to ensure the guest's satisfaction. Demonstrating your dedication to resolving problems will not only salvage the guest's experience but also showcase your commitment to continuous improvement.

In conclusion, attracting positive reviews and building a strong reputation is essential for success in the realm of Airbnb property flipping. By prioritizing exceptional guest experiences, effective communication, and proactive management of feedback, you can establish yourself as a trusted and sought-after host. With a strong reputation and an abundance of positive reviews, your Airbnb property flipping business is bound to thrive.

Utilizing Social Media and Other Marketing Channels

In today's digital age, harnessing the power of social media and other marketing channels is essential for real estate investors looking to succeed in the niche of Airbnb property flipping. With the rise of platforms like Airbnb, purchasing distressed properties, renovating them, and listing them on Airbnb for short-term rentals has become an increasingly popular investment strategy. However, with the competition growing, it is crucial to stand out from the crowd and reach potential guests effectively. This subchapter will explore the various ways real estate investors can leverage social media and other marketing channels to maximize their success in Airbnb property flipping.

Social media platforms such as Facebook, Instagram, and Twitter offer incredible opportunities for real estate investors to showcase their properties and engage with potential guests. By creating compelling content, including high-quality photos and videos of the renovated properties, investors can attract attention and generate interest in their listings. Additionally, utilizing targeted advertising on these platforms can help reach a specific audience interested in short-term rentals, increasing the chances of securing bookings.

Another effective marketing channel for Airbnb property flipping is email marketing. Building an email list of potential guests allows investors to directly communicate with interested parties, providing updates on new properties, special offers, and other valuable information. By crafting engaging email campaigns and offering incentives, such as discounts or exclusive access to certain properties, investors can build a loyal customer base and secure repeat bookings.

Furthermore, collaborating with influencers and bloggers within the real estate and travel industry can be a game-changer for marketing Airbnb properties. Partnering with influential individuals who have a significant following can expose the listings to a wider audience, increasing visibility and bookings. Additionally, engaging in guest blogging opportunities and providing valuable content on popular real estate and travel websites can establish credibility and attract potential guests.

In conclusion, real estate investors specializing in Airbnb property flipping must embrace the power of social media and other marketing channels to succeed in a competitive market. By utilizing platforms like Facebook, Instagram, and Twitter, as well as implementing email marketing campaigns and collaborating with influencers, investors can effectively market their properties and maximize their chances of securing bookings. Staying ahead of the competition requires continuous innovation and adaptability, and incorporating these marketing strategies will undoubtedly set investors on the path from distressed to deluxe in their Airbnb property flipping journey.

Chapter 7: Managing Airbnb Rentals

Setting Up Efficient Operations and Systems

In the fast-paced world of Airbnb property flipping, efficiency is the key to success. As a real estate investor specializing in purchasing distressed properties, renovating them, and then listing them on Airbnb for short-term rentals, it is crucial to set up efficient operations and systems to maximize your profitability and minimize your efforts. This subchapter will provide you with essential guidelines on how to streamline your operations and implement efficient systems to ensure a smooth and profitable property flipping experience.

The first step in setting up efficient operations is to establish a well-defined process for property acquisition. This includes conducting thorough market research to identify distressed properties with high potential for renovation and profitability. Additionally, developing relationships with local real estate agents, contractors, and suppliers can help expedite the property acquisition process and ensure competitive pricing for renovations.

Once you have acquired a property, it is essential to implement efficient renovation processes. This involves creating a detailed project plan, setting realistic timelines, and closely managing contractors to ensure projects are completed on time and within budget. By establishing clear communication channels and regularly monitoring progress, you can avoid costly delays and ensure the successful execution of your renovation projects.

Efficiency in the listing and management of your Airbnb properties is also crucial. Implementing a streamlined process for property listing, including professional photography and compelling descriptions, can significantly increase your booking rates. Moreover, utilizing property management software or hiring a reliable property manager can help automate tasks such as guest communication, check-ins, and cleaning, freeing up your time to focus on growing your property portfolio.

Another vital aspect of efficient operations is optimizing your pricing strategy. By analyzing market trends, demand patterns, and competitor pricing, you can set competitive rates that maximize your occupancy rates and rental income. Utilizing dynamic pricing tools or hiring a professional pricing strategist can help you stay ahead of the competition and adapt to changing market conditions.

Lastly, implementing efficient systems for financial management and tracking is essential for maintaining profitability. Utilizing accounting software or hiring a bookkeeper can help you accurately track expenses, monitor cash flow, and ensure compliance with tax regulations.

By setting up efficient operations and systems, you can streamline your property flipping process, increase profitability, and gain a competitive edge in the Airbnb property flipping niche. Embracing technology, establishing clear processes, and focusing on continuous improvement will position you as a successful real estate investor in the exciting world of Airbnb property flipping.

Handling Guest Communication and Bookings

In the world of Airbnb property flipping, effective guest communication and seamless bookings can make all the difference between a successful venture and a mediocre one. As real estate investors, it is crucial to understand the importance of building strong relationships with guests and streamlining the booking process to maximize profits and ensure repeat business. This subchapter will delve into the key strategies for handling guest communication and bookings to transform distressed properties into deluxe Airbnb rentals.

1. Prompt and Professional Communication: Timely and professional communication with potential guests is essential for creating a positive first impression. Responding promptly to inquiries, being polite and helpful, and addressing any concerns or questions can go a long way in building trust and establishing a solid reputation in the Airbnb community. Utilizing automation tools, such as templates and pre-set messages, can help streamline communication without sacrificing personalization.

2. Creating an Attractive Listing:
Investing time and effort into creating an appealing listing is crucial for attracting potential guests. High-quality photos, a detailed description of the property's features and amenities, and highlighting any unique selling points can greatly increase the chances of securing bookings. Additionally, regularly updating the listing with accurate availability and pricing information ensures transparency and avoids potential misunderstandings.

3. Implementing a Smooth Booking Process:
Simplifying the booking process can enhance the guest experience and lead to higher conversion rates. Offering instant booking options and providing clear instructions on how to complete the reservation can eliminate unnecessary hurdles and encourage guests to proceed with their bookings. Utilizing a reliable booking management system can also help streamline the process and minimize administrative tasks.

4. Setting Clear Expectations:
Clear and concise communication regarding house rules, check-in/check-out procedures, and any additional charges or fees is vital for ensuring a smooth guest experience. Guests should have a comprehensive understanding of what to expect during their stay to avoid any potential misunderstandings or conflicts. Utilizing welcome guides or digital manuals can provide guests with all the necessary information and enhance their overall satisfaction.

5. Proactive Communication and Feedback:
Maintaining open communication with guests throughout their stay can help address any issues or concerns promptly. Sending follow-up messages to ensure their satisfaction and encouraging them to leave reviews can help build a positive reputation and attract future guests. Taking guest feedback into account and continuously improving the property based on their suggestions can lead to higher occupancy rates and increased profitability.

By implementing these strategies, real estate investors specializing in Airbnb property flipping can establish themselves as trusted hosts and maximize their profits. Effective guest communication and streamlined bookings are the foundations for transforming distressed properties into deluxe accommodations that will attract a continuous stream of satisfied guests.

Cleaning and Maintenance Strategies

When it comes to Airbnb property flipping, ensuring that your properties are clean and well-maintained is of utmost importance. In this subchapter, we will discuss some effective cleaning and maintenance strategies that will help you attract more guests, receive positive reviews, and maximize your return on investment.

1. Regular Cleaning Schedule: Establishing a regular cleaning schedule is crucial to maintaining the cleanliness and hygiene of your property. Depending on the turnover frequency, consider hiring professional cleaners or a reliable cleaning service to thoroughly clean the property between guests. This will help create a positive first impression and ensure that your guests have a comfortable and enjoyable stay.

2. Attention to Detail: Paying attention to every detail of your property is a key aspect of successful Airbnb property flipping. Make sure to clean not only the obvious areas but also those easily overlooked, such as baseboards, light switches, and door handles. Additionally, check for any damages or maintenance issues and address them promptly to avoid negative reviews and dissatisfied guests.

3. Quality Linens and Amenities: Providing high-quality linens and amenities can significantly enhance the guest experience. Invest in comfortable mattresses, soft bedding, and plush towels to create a luxurious atmosphere. Additionally, offer essential amenities such as toiletries, coffee, and tea, to make your guests feel welcome and cared for.

4. Efficient Communication: Establishing efficient communication channels with your guests is crucial for addressing any cleaning or maintenance concerns promptly. Respond to their inquiries or complaints in a timely manner, and be proactive in resolving any issues that may arise during their stay. This will not only ensure guest satisfaction but also help you maintain a positive reputation as a responsive and attentive host.

5. Regular Maintenance Checks: Conduct regular maintenance checks to identify any potential issues before they escalate. This includes inspecting plumbing, electrical systems, HVAC units, and appliances. By addressing maintenance concerns early on, you can prevent costly repairs and ensure that your property remains in top-notch condition.

Remember, as an Airbnb property flipper, your goal is to create a seamless and enjoyable experience for your guests. By implementing effective cleaning and maintenance strategies, you can significantly increase the likelihood of positive reviews, repeat bookings, and ultimately, maximize your profits.

Dealing with Difficult Guests and Situations

As a real estate investor specializing in Airbnb property flipping, it is essential to have a solid plan for dealing with difficult guests and situations. While the majority of guests will be pleasant and respectful, there may be instances where you encounter challenging individuals or unexpected issues. In this subchapter, we will explore effective strategies to navigate these situations and ensure a positive experience for both you and your guests.

1. Setting Clear Expectations: Communication is key when it comes to avoiding misunderstandings and potential conflicts. Prior to arrival, make sure to provide guests with detailed house rules, check-in procedures, and any other relevant information. By setting clear expectations, you can minimize the risk of difficult situations arising.

2. Screening Guests: One way to mitigate potential issues is by implementing a screening process for guests. This can involve conducting background checks, verifying identification, and reviewing previous guest reviews. By carefully vetting guests, you can minimize the likelihood of problematic individuals staying at your property.

3. Addressing Issues Promptly: Despite your best efforts, there may be times when issues arise during a guest's stay. It is crucial to address these problems promptly and professionally. Actively listen to the guest's concerns and work towards finding a satisfactory solution. By addressing issues in a timely manner, you can prevent them from escalating into larger problems.

4. Building a Support Network: As an Airbnb property flipper, it is beneficial to establish a network of reliable professionals to assist you in managing difficult situations. This network may include local maintenance teams, cleaning services, or even legal counsel. Having trusted individuals on hand can provide peace of mind and streamline the resolution process.

5. Implementing a Guest Review System: Encourage guests to leave reviews of their stay. This feedback not only helps you improve your property but also serves as a reference for potential guests. By implementing a review system, you can gain valuable insights into the experiences of previous guests, allowing you to identify any recurring issues and take proactive measures.

6. Maintaining a Positive Attitude: Dealing with difficult guests and situations can be challenging, but maintaining a positive attitude is crucial. Remember that these situations are an opportunity for growth and improvement. By approaching challenges with a proactive mindset, you can turn them into valuable learning experiences.

In conclusion, by proactively addressing difficult guests and situations, you can maintain a positive Airbnb property flipping experience. Setting clear expectations, screening guests, addressing issues promptly, building a support network, implementing a guest review system, and maintaining a positive attitude are all indispensable strategies for navigating potential challenges. By mastering these techniques, you can ensure a successful venture in the world of Airbnb property flipping.

Chapter 8: Maximizing Profit and Scaling your Airbnb Property Flipping Business

Analyzing Financial Performance and Return on Investment

In the fast-paced world of real estate investing, it is crucial for Airbnb property flippers to be well-versed in analyzing financial performance and return on investment. This subchapter will delve into the essential aspects that real estate investors need to consider when evaluating the profitability of their Airbnb property flipping ventures.

One of the primary indicators of financial performance is the return on investment (ROI). ROI allows investors to measure the efficiency of their investment by comparing the gains or losses relative to the initial investment. In the context of Airbnb property flipping, ROI provides insights into the profitability of purchasing distressed properties, renovating them, and subsequently listing them on Airbnb for short-term rentals.

To calculate ROI accurately, investors must consider various elements. Firstly, the initial purchase price of the distressed property needs to be factored in. Additionally, renovation costs, including materials, labor, and any necessary permits, should be carefully accounted for. Other expenses, such as property taxes, insurance, and marketing fees, also play a role in determining the total investment amount.

On the revenue side, investors need to analyze the potential rental income generated from the Airbnb listings. This entails considering the average daily rate, occupancy rate, and the number of days throughout the year that the property is expected to be rented out. By multiplying these factors, investors can estimate the annual rental income.

Once the total investment and rental income figures are determined, calculating ROI becomes straightforward. By dividing the net profit (rental income minus expenses) by the total investment and multiplying the result by 100, investors can assess the percentage ROI.

In addition to ROI, it is crucial for real estate investors to evaluate other financial performance metrics. These may include gross rental yield, cash-on-cash return, and capitalization rate. Each metric provides a different perspective on the profitability and potential return of the investment.

By thoroughly analyzing the financial performance and return on investment of their Airbnb property flipping projects, real estate investors can make informed decisions and maximize their profits. Understanding these metrics allows investors to identify areas for improvement, adjust their strategies, and ultimately achieve success in the niche of Airbnb property flipping.

Strategies for Increasing Occupancy Rates and Revenue

As a real estate investor specializing in Airbnb property flipping, your ultimate goal is to maximize occupancy rates and revenue from your short-term rental properties. In this subchapter, we will explore various strategies that can help you achieve these objectives and turn distressed properties into deluxe Airbnb listings.

1. Optimize Your Listing: The first step in increasing occupancy rates and revenue is to create an attractive and compelling listing. Invest time in professional photography, write a detailed and engaging description, highlight the unique features of your property, and ensure that your listing is optimized for search engines. By standing out from the competition, you will attract more potential guests.

2. Set Competitive Pricing: Pricing plays a crucial role in attracting guests and maximizing revenue. Conduct market research to understand the pricing trends in your area and set competitive rates. Consider factors such as location, amenities, and seasonality, and adjust your pricing accordingly. Additionally, offering discounts for longer stays or off-peak periods can help attract more bookings.

3. Enhance Guest Experience: Providing an exceptional guest experience is key to increasing occupancy rates and receiving positive reviews. Ensure that your property is clean, well-maintained, and equipped with essential amenities. Consider adding extras such as high-speed internet, smart home technology, or thoughtful touches like welcome baskets. Promptly responding to guest inquiries and addressing any issues that arise during their stay will also contribute to positive reviews and repeat bookings.

4. Utilize Dynamic Pricing: Dynamic pricing tools can help you adjust your rates in real-time based on factors such as demand, local events, and competitor rates. By utilizing these tools, you can optimize your pricing to maximize revenue during peak periods and attract more guests during low-demand periods.

5. Invest in Marketing: In order to increase occupancy rates, it is essential to promote your listing effectively. Utilize various marketing channels such as social media, online travel agencies, and local tourism websites. Consider running targeted advertising campaigns to reach your ideal audience and increase visibility. Building a strong online presence and maintaining positive guest reviews will also help to attract more bookings.

6. Offer Unique Experiences: Differentiate your property by offering unique experiences to your guests. Consider partnering with local businesses to provide exclusive discounts or packages for your guests. Additionally, providing a personalized guidebook with recommendations for nearby attractions, restaurants, and activities will enhance the guest experience and encourage positive reviews.

By implementing these strategies, you can increase occupancy rates and revenue for your Airbnb property flipping business. Remember that consistent monitoring and adaptability are key to staying competitive in the ever-evolving short-term rental market.

Expanding your Airbnb Property Portfolio

As a real estate investor with a niche in Airbnb property flipping, purchasing distressed properties, renovating them, and then listing them on Airbnb for short-term rentals can be a lucrative venture. However, once you have successfully flipped a few properties, you may start wondering how to expand your Airbnb property portfolio and take your business to new heights. In this subchapter, we will explore some strategies and tips to help you do just that.

1. Research and Identify Potential Markets: The first step in expanding your Airbnb property portfolio is to research and identify potential markets where short-term rentals are in high demand. Look for cities or neighborhoods with high tourism rates, business conferences, or other events that attract travelers. Analyze data on occupancy rates, average rental income, and regulations to ensure you choose a market that aligns with your investment goals.

2. Network and Collaborate: Building a strong network of real estate professionals, property managers, and fellow investors can open doors to new opportunities. Attend industry conferences, join online forums, and participate in local real estate associations to meet like-minded individuals. Collaborating with others can help you find off-market deals, gain valuable insights, and even pool resources for joint ventures.

3. Secure Financing: Expanding your Airbnb property portfolio requires adequate financing. Evaluate your financial position and explore different funding options such as traditional bank loans, private lenders, or partnerships. Keep in mind that having a solid business plan and a track record of successful Airbnb flips will increase your chances of securing favorable financing terms.

4. Streamline Operations: As you expand your portfolio, managing multiple properties can become overwhelming. Streamline your operations by implementing efficient systems and processes. Consider leveraging technology, such as property management software, to automate tasks like booking, guest communication, and maintenance requests. Hiring a reliable property manager can also help alleviate the workload.

5. Continuously Educate Yourself: The real estate industry is constantly evolving, and staying informed about market trends, regulations, and innovative strategies is crucial. Invest in your education by attending workshops, webinars, and training programs specific to Airbnb property flipping. This will help you stay ahead of the competition and make informed decisions when expanding your portfolio.

Expanding your Airbnb property portfolio requires careful planning, research, and a solid understanding of the market. By following these strategies and staying committed to continuous learning, you can successfully grow your Airbnb property flipping business and achieve long-term success in the real estate investment industry.

Exit Strategies: Selling or Holding Properties

When it comes to Airbnb property flipping, one of the most crucial decisions investors face is determining the appropriate exit strategy for their investments. Two popular options that investors often consider are selling the property or holding onto it for long-term gains. In this subchapter, we will delve into the advantages and considerations of each strategy to help real estate investors make informed decisions.

Selling a property can offer a quick return on investment, especially in a hot real estate market. By flipping the property and listing it on Airbnb for short-term rentals, investors can generate substantial cash flow in a short period. This strategy allows for a quick turnover of funds, which can be reinvested into other distressed properties, thus expanding the portfolio. Additionally, selling a property eliminates the potential risks associated with long-term property ownership, such as maintenance costs and market fluctuations.

However, before rushing into a sale, investors must consider several factors. Firstly, it is crucial to analyze the current market conditions and determine if it is a seller's market, where prices are high, or a buyer's market, where prices are more competitive. Proper market research ensures that investors sell their properties at the optimal time, maximizing profits. Additionally, investors should evaluate their financial goals and determine if a quick return on investment aligns with their long-term objectives.

On the other hand, holding properties for long-term gains can also be a lucrative strategy for Airbnb property flipping investors. By holding onto a property, investors can benefit from capital appreciation, rental income, and tax advantages. Additionally, investors have the opportunity to ride out market fluctuations and potentially sell the property at a higher price when the market is favorable.

When considering the holding strategy, investors must carefully assess the property's potential for long-term appreciation and its rental income potential. Conducting a thorough analysis of the local real estate market, projected growth, and rental demand is crucial to make an informed decision. Additionally, investors should evaluate their financial capacity to maintain the property for an extended period, including expenses such as mortgage payments, property taxes, and maintenance costs.

Ultimately, the decision to sell or hold a property depends on the investor's financial goals, market conditions, and risk tolerance. Real estate investors in the Airbnb property flipping niche must weigh the advantages and considerations of each strategy before making a well-informed choice. By carefully evaluating these factors, investors can optimize their returns and build a successful portfolio in the dynamic world of Airbnb property flipping.

Chapter 9: Overcoming Common Challenges and Pitfalls

Dealing with Legal and Regulatory Issues

In the world of real estate investment, the path to success is often fraught with legal and regulatory challenges. As Airbnb property flipping gains popularity among investors, it is crucial to understand the legal considerations and navigate the regulatory landscape effectively. This chapter will equip real estate investors in the niche of Airbnb property flipping with the knowledge and strategies required to overcome these hurdles and thrive in their ventures.

One of the primary legal issues faced by Airbnb property flippers relates to property zoning. Each city has its own zoning regulations that determine the permitted uses of properties within different areas. It is essential to thoroughly research and understand the zoning laws in the target location to ensure that short-term rentals are allowed. Additionally, obtaining the necessary permits and licenses may be required, depending on local ordinances. This subchapter will provide insights on how to navigate zoning laws and acquire the required permits, ensuring compliance with local regulations.

Another significant legal consideration is the legal agreement between the property owner and Airbnb. Investors must be well-versed in the terms and conditions set forth by Airbnb and understand their obligations as hosts. This subchapter will outline key points to consider when entering into agreements with Airbnb, ensuring a smooth and legally compliant partnership.

Additionally, taxation is a crucial aspect of any real estate investment. Airbnb property flipping introduces unique tax implications, such as income tax, occupancy tax, and sales tax. This subchapter will provide guidance on understanding and managing these tax obligations, including strategies to maximize deductions and minimize tax liabilities.

Furthermore, it is essential to address liability concerns when engaging in short-term rentals. Understanding insurance requirements and implementing proper risk management strategies are vital to protect both the investor's assets and the well-being of guests. This subchapter will provide insights on insurance options and best practices for mitigating potential liabilities.

Lastly, in the ever-evolving landscape of short-term rentals, it is crucial to stay updated with the latest legal and regulatory changes. This subchapter will highlight the importance of ongoing education and awareness of any new laws or regulations that may affect Airbnb property flipping.

By addressing these legal and regulatory issues head-on, real estate investors in the niche of Airbnb property flipping can confidently navigate the complexities of the industry. Armed with the knowledge and strategies provided in this subchapter, investors will be well-equipped to overcome challenges, ensure legal compliance, and maximize their success in the world of Airbnb property flipping.

Managing Cash Flow and Financial Risks

One of the most crucial aspects of successful Airbnb property flipping is effectively managing cash flow and financial risks. As a real estate investor engaged in the niche of purchasing distressed properties, renovating them, and listing them on Airbnb for short-term rentals, it is essential to have a solid understanding of cash flow management and risk mitigation strategies. This subchapter will provide you with valuable insights and practical tips to help you navigate the financial aspects of your Airbnb property flipping business.

To begin with, maintaining a healthy cash flow is vital for the sustainability and growth of your business. Flipping properties requires significant upfront investments, including the purchase price, renovations, and operational expenses. It is crucial to accurately estimate your costs and create a comprehensive budget that considers all potential expenses. This includes not only the obvious expenses such as property acquisition and renovation costs but also often overlooked expenses like property taxes, insurance, utilities, and marketing expenses.

Moreover, it is essential to have a robust financial management system in place. This includes maintaining accurate and up-to-date records of income and expenses, tracking your cash flow on a regular basis, and analyzing financial statements to identify potential areas for improvement. Utilizing accounting software or hiring a professional bookkeeper can greatly simplify this process and provide you with the necessary insights to make informed financial decisions.

In addition to managing cash flow, it is crucial to mitigate financial risks associated with your Airbnb property flipping business. This includes identifying and managing potential risks such as property market fluctuations, unforeseen renovation expenses, and legal and regulatory challenges. Conducting thorough due diligence before purchasing distressed properties, working with reliable contractors, and staying updated on local regulations can help minimize these risks.

Furthermore, it is advisable to have a contingency plan in place for unexpected events that may impact your cash flow. This can include setting aside a reserve fund to cover unforeseen expenses or having alternative financing options available in case of emergencies.

By effectively managing your cash flow and mitigating financial risks, you can ensure the long-term success of your Airbnb property flipping business. This subchapter will equip you with the necessary knowledge and strategies to make informed financial decisions, maintain a healthy cash flow, and protect your investment. With careful planning and diligent execution, you can turn distressed properties into profitable Airbnb rentals and achieve financial success in the real estate market.

Navigating Market Fluctuations and Economic Factors

In the fast-paced world of real estate investing, understanding and effectively navigating market fluctuations and economic factors is crucial to achieving success. This subchapter will delve into the strategies and insights necessary for real estate investors, particularly those in the niche of Airbnb property flipping, to thrive in an ever-changing market.

Market fluctuations can be both a blessing and a curse for real estate investors. On one hand, they provide opportunities for savvy investors to purchase distressed properties at a lower cost. However, these fluctuations also pose risks, as they can impact property values and rental demand. To mitigate these risks, it is essential to stay informed about current market trends and economic indicators that could influence the profitability of your Airbnb property flipping venture.

When analyzing market fluctuations, it is important to consider both local and global economic factors. Local factors such as job growth, population trends, and infrastructure developments can significantly impact the demand for short-term rentals in a particular area. Additionally, global economic factors like interest rates, inflation, and geopolitical events can have ripple effects on the real estate market as a whole.

To navigate market fluctuations successfully, real estate investors should adopt a proactive approach. This involves conducting thorough market research, staying updated on economic news, and building a network of professionals who can provide insights and guidance. By doing so, investors can identify emerging trends, anticipate shifts in rental demand, and make informed decisions about purchasing and renovating distressed properties.

Moreover, it is crucial to develop a flexible investment strategy that accounts for potential market fluctuations. This may involve diversifying your property portfolio across different locations, adjusting rental rates based on demand, or considering alternative uses for your properties in the event of a downturn.

In summary, understanding and navigating market fluctuations and economic factors are essential skills for real estate investors in the niche of Airbnb property flipping. By staying informed, adopting a proactive approach, and developing a flexible investment strategy, investors can capitalize on market opportunities, mitigate risks, and achieve long-term success in this dynamic industry.

Learning from Mistakes and Continuous Improvement

In the fast-paced world of real estate investing, it is crucial for Airbnb property flippers to embrace a mindset of learning from mistakes and striving for continuous improvement. This subchapter will delve into the importance of recognizing and analyzing mistakes, and how to implement strategies that lead to ongoing growth and success.

Mistakes are an inevitable part of any business venture, and Airbnb property flipping is no exception. However, what sets successful investors apart is their ability to view mistakes as valuable learning opportunities. By carefully analyzing every misstep, investors can identify the root causes and develop effective strategies to prevent similar errors in the future.

One common mistake made by Airbnb property flippers is underestimating the renovation costs. In the pursuit of maximizing profits, investors often fall into the trap of cutting corners or overlooking crucial aspects of the renovation process. By acknowledging and understanding this mistake, investors can implement a comprehensive budgeting system that accounts for all potential expenses, ensuring a more accurate estimation of costs.

Another crucial aspect of continuous improvement is staying updated with the latest trends and industry best practices. Real estate markets and Airbnb regulations are constantly evolving, and it is vital for investors to stay ahead of the curve. By actively seeking out educational resources, attending seminars, and networking with other experienced flippers, investors can stay informed and adapt their strategies accordingly.

Furthermore, maintaining open lines of communication with guests and actively seeking feedback is essential for ongoing improvement. By listening to guest reviews and suggestions, investors can identify areas for improvement in terms of amenities, customer service, and overall guest experience. Implementing these improvements not only enhances guest satisfaction but also boosts positive reviews, which can significantly impact the success of future rentals.

Lastly, investors should establish a culture of continuous learning within their team. Encouraging employees to seek ongoing education and providing opportunities for professional development can lead to a more knowledgeable and motivated workforce. By investing in their team's growth, investors create a positive work environment that fosters innovation and ensures continuous improvement.

In conclusion, learning from mistakes and embracing continuous improvement are fundamental to success in the realm of Airbnb property flipping. By recognizing and analyzing mistakes, staying updated with industry trends, actively seeking guest feedback, and investing in team development, investors can enhance their strategies, maximize profits, and create a sustainable business model. With a commitment to self-improvement, even distressed properties can be transformed into deluxe Airbnb rentals that attract and delight guests.

Chapter 10: Conclusion and Next Steps

Recap of Key Strategies and Takeaways

As real estate investors, the world of Airbnb property flipping presents a unique opportunity to acquire distressed properties, transform them into deluxe accommodations, and list them on Airbnb for short-term rentals. Throughout this book, "From Distressed to Deluxe: Airbnb Property Flipping Strategies for Investors," we have explored a range of strategies and takeaways to help you succeed in this niche market.

One of the key strategies we have discussed is the importance of location. Purchasing distressed properties in prime locations can significantly increase your chances of attracting high-paying Airbnb guests. Investing in properties near popular tourist attractions, business districts, or vibrant neighborhoods will ensure a steady flow of bookings and maximize your rental income potential.

Another crucial aspect of Airbnb property flipping is the renovation process. We have outlined various renovation strategies that can transform distressed properties into deluxe accommodations. From upgrading the kitchen and bathrooms to enhancing the curb appeal, ensuring that your property stands out from the competition is essential. Additionally, incorporating modern amenities such as smart home technology, high-speed internet, and comfortable furnishings can significantly increase your property's appeal to potential guests.

To excel in this niche market, it is vital to understand the dynamics of Airbnb pricing and optimizing your rental income. We have discussed various pricing strategies, such as dynamic pricing algorithms and seasonal adjustments, that can help you maximize your occupancy rate and profitability. Effective property management is also crucial, whether you choose to self-manage or hire a professional management company. Maintaining excellent guest reviews and providing exceptional customer service are essential for long-term success.

Furthermore, we have emphasized the significance of marketing and branding your Airbnb property effectively. Creating a compelling listing with professional photos, engaging descriptions, and highlighting unique features can attract the attention of potential guests. Leveraging social media platforms, online travel agencies, and local partnerships can also help generate more bookings and establish your property as a top choice for travelers.

In conclusion, successfully flipping distressed properties into deluxe Airbnb accommodations requires a comprehensive approach that encompasses strategic purchasing, renovation, pricing, property management, and marketing. By implementing the key strategies and takeaways outlined in this book, real estate investors can tap into the lucrative niche of Airbnb property flipping and achieve remarkable success. Keep learning, adapting, and staying ahead of the market trends to maximize your returns and establish a thriving portfolio of Airbnb properties.

Developing a Personal Action Plan

In the world of real estate investment, success often lies in the ability to create and execute a well-defined action plan. This is especially true for real estate investors specializing in Airbnb property flipping – a niche that involves purchasing distressed properties, renovating them, and then listing them on Airbnb for short-term rentals. To achieve optimal results in this competitive market, it is essential for investors to develop a personal action plan tailored to their specific goals and circumstances.

The first step in creating a personal action plan is to define your investment objectives. Are you looking to generate short-term cash flow or build long-term wealth? Understanding your goals will help you align your actions accordingly. Additionally, it is important to consider your financial resources and risk tolerance when determining the scope and scale of your investment activities.

Once your objectives are clear, the next step is to conduct thorough market research. Familiarize yourself with the local real estate market, including popular Airbnb destinations, rental rates, occupancy rates, and competition. This information will guide your property selection process and ensure you invest in areas with high demand and potential for profitability.

With a solid understanding of the market, it is time to develop a property acquisition strategy. This includes identifying distressed properties that offer the greatest potential for value appreciation through renovation and subsequent short-term rental. Consider working with experienced real estate agents or professionals specializing in distressed properties to expand your network and gain access to off-market deals.

As you acquire properties, it is crucial to establish a comprehensive renovation plan. This should include a detailed budget, timeline, and a list of contractors or service providers. Choose renovations that will attract Airbnb guests, such as modern amenities, stylish interiors, and enhanced security features. Balancing cost-efficiency with quality will maximize your return on investment.

Once the properties are renovated and ready for listing on Airbnb, it is time to develop a marketing strategy to attract potential guests. This may involve professional photography, engaging property descriptions, competitive pricing, and utilizing social media platforms to reach a wider audience. Monitoring guest reviews and feedback will enable you to continuously improve your properties and enhance the guest experience.

Finally, it is important to regularly evaluate the performance of your investments and adjust your action plan accordingly. Keep track of financial metrics such as occupancy rates, rental income, and expenses to assess the profitability of each property. This data-driven approach will help you make informed decisions on property acquisitions, renovations, and overall business growth.

In conclusion, developing a personal action plan is crucial for real estate investors specializing in Airbnb property flipping. By defining your goals, conducting thorough market research, implementing effective property acquisition and renovation strategies, and continuously evaluating performance, you can maximize your success in this niche and transform distressed properties into deluxe short-term rentals.

Resources and Further Reading for Real Estate Investors.

Resources and Further Reading for Real Estate Investors

As a real estate investor in the niche of Airbnb property flipping, it is crucial to stay informed and continually educate yourself on the latest trends, strategies, and resources available to help you succeed in this competitive market. In this subchapter, we will explore some valuable resources and further reading materials that can assist you in your journey from purchasing distressed properties to renovating them and listing them on Airbnb for short-term rentals.

1. "The Airbnb Story: How Three Ordinary Guys Disrupted an Industry, Made Billions...and Created Plenty of Controversy" by Leigh Gallagher: This book provides an in-depth look into the rise of Airbnb and its impact on the real estate industry. It offers valuable insights into the sharing economy and how you can leverage Airbnb's platform to maximize your investments.

2. "The Book on Rental Property Investing" by Brandon Turner: Although not specific to Airbnb, this book is a must-read for any real estate investor. It covers essential topics such as property selection, financing, and managing rental properties, providing a solid foundation for your real estate endeavors.

3. Real estate investment forums and online communities: Connecting with fellow real estate investors on platforms like BiggerPockets, REI Club, or Reddit's real estate investing subreddit can provide invaluable networking opportunities, advice, and insights from experienced investors in the Airbnb property flipping niche.

4. Airbnb's website and resources: Airbnb offers a wealth of information for hosts and property owners. Explore their blog, community center, and resource library to learn about best practices, regulations, and tips for optimizing your property listings.

5. Local real estate investment associations: Joining local real estate investment associations or attending meetups can help you build a network of like-minded individuals and stay up-to-date with local market trends and opportunities.

6. Online courses and educational platforms: Platforms like Udemy, Coursera, and LinkedIn Learning offer a wide range of real estate investing courses. Look for courses specifically tailored to Airbnb property flipping or related topics such as property management, interior design, and marketing.

7. Industry publications and blogs: Stay informed about the latest news and insights in the real estate industry by reading publications like Forbes Real Estate, The Wall Street Journal's Real Estate section, or blogs like Mashvisor and Rentberry's Airbnb blog.

Remember, continuous learning and staying informed are essential for success in the ever-evolving real estate market. By utilizing these resources and further reading materials, you can enhance your knowledge and skills, ultimately increasing your chances of achieving profitability and success in the Airbnb property flipping niche.

From Distressed to Deluxe: Airbnb Property Flipping Strategies for Investors

"....is for real estate investors who are specifically interested in Airbnb property flipping. This book is tailored to those investors who are keen on purchasing distressed properties, renovating them, and then listing them on Airbnb for short-term rentals."

Clyde N. Cook, III

Entrepeneur, Real Estate Investor, Certified Private Money Broker, Author, Certified Credit Repair Specialist.

www.ingramcontent.com/pod-product-compliance
Lightning Source LLC
LaVergne TN
LVHW022058200926
848481LV00003B/979
9798215393307